Wild and Free

Mick Manning and Brita Granström

W

FRANKLIN WATTS

LONDON • SYDNEY

Tigers are protected - but they could still become extinct unless poachers are stopped.

2

Who could live in a world without tigers?

Not Gita! Gita lives in India. She has only
seen tigers in books, but she needs to know
they are out there – living with their
cubs in the dark forests.
Wild and free.

Who could live in a world without sharks?

Not Lee-Anne!
Lee-Anne lives in the USA and she thinks sharks are cool – sharp fins slicing through the oceans.
Wild and free.

White sharks are becoming very rare. They are usually harmless to humans but sometimes mistake swimmers for their favourite food – seals.

Who could live
in a world without wildcats?

Not Angus! Angus lives in Britain and
dreams of seeing a wildcat someday –
leaping through the windy heather.
Wild and free.

Wildcats are meeting tame cats and breeding with them – this means that soon there may be very few true wildcats left.

7

Who could live in a world without whales?

Not Atsku! Atsku lives in Japan. She wants to go on a whale-spotting holiday to see them – such huge animals, breaking the waves.
Wild and free.

Whale numbers are growing now, but whales still need protection.

9

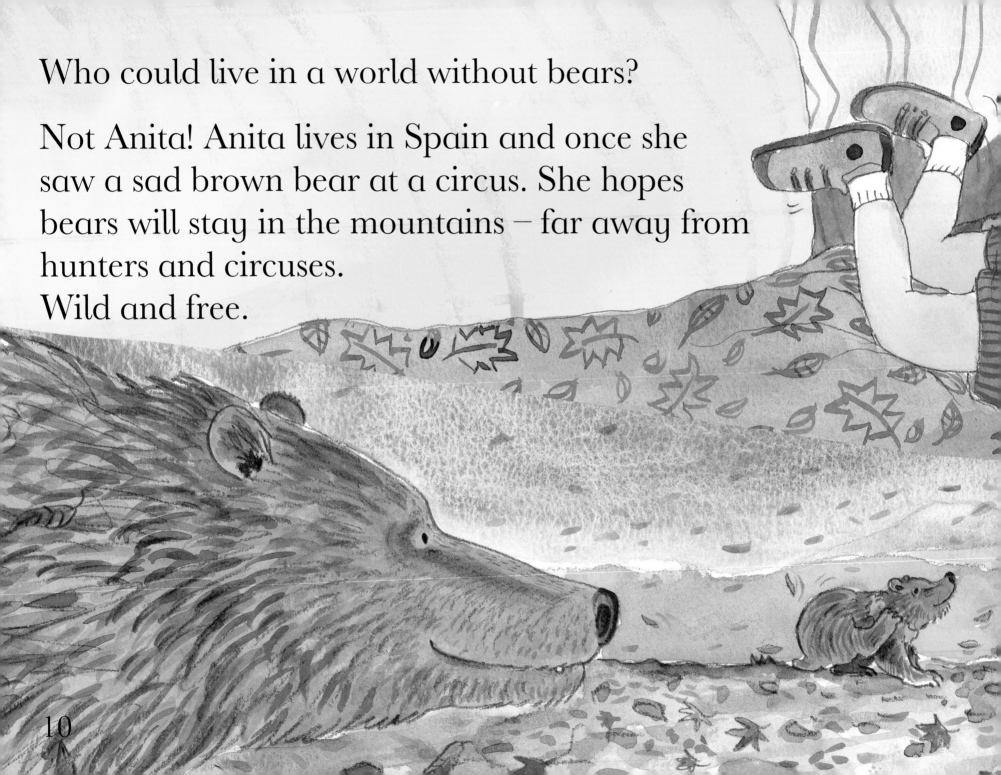

Who could live in a world without bears?

Not Anita! Anita lives in Spain and once she saw a sad brown bear at a circus. She hopes bears will stay in the mountains – far away from hunters and circuses.
Wild and free.

There are a few bears left in some European countries, they are extinct in many others.

Who could live in a world without gorillas?

Not Essi! Essi lives in Africa and her ambition
is to see a silverback gorilla – swinging a
toddler in his arms.
Wild and free.

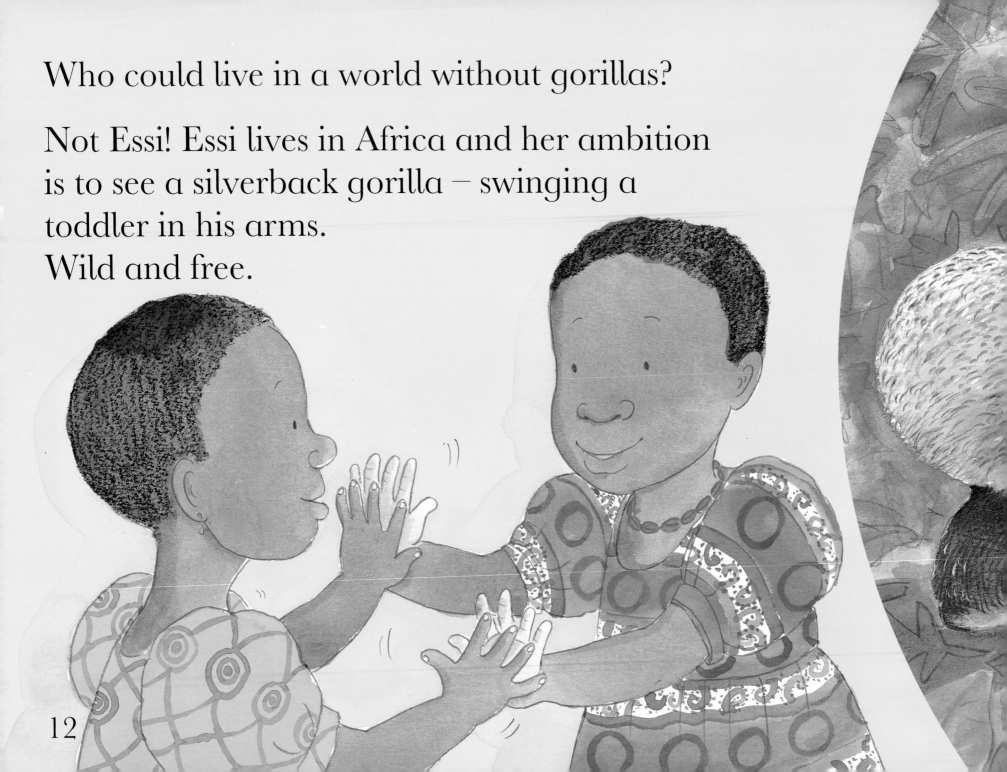

Who could live in a world without rhinoceroses?

Not Mo! Mo lives in Africa and he hopes to see a rhino one day. A rhino with a huge horn on her nose and a small calf by her side – gallumphing across the plains.
Wild and free.

15

Who could live in a world without cougars?

Not Jake! Jake lives in Canada.
Sometimes he imagines
he really is a cougar –
a golden cat padding
through the Rocky
Mountains.
Wild and free.

Cougars or mountain lions are shot because they sometimes kill cattle and sheep.

Who could live in a world without koalas?

Not Luke! Luke lives in Australia and goes to sleep dreaming about koalas – shinning up the trees carrying their babies 'piggy-back'.
Wild and free.

The eucalyptus trees koalas need for food are disappearing. Other dangers include bush fires and dogs on the hunt.

19

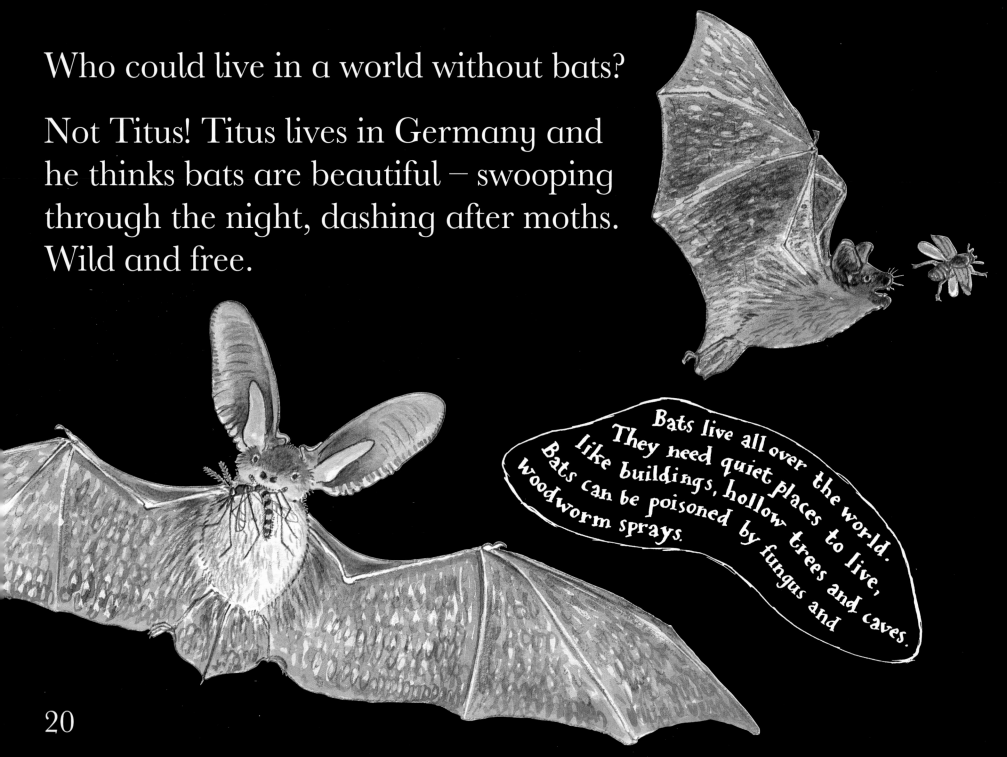

Who could live in a world without bats?

Not Titus! Titus lives in Germany and he thinks bats are beautiful – swooping through the night, dashing after moths. Wild and free.

Bats live all over the world. They need quiet places to live, like buildings, hollow trees and caves. Bats can be poisoned by fungus and woodworm sprays.

20

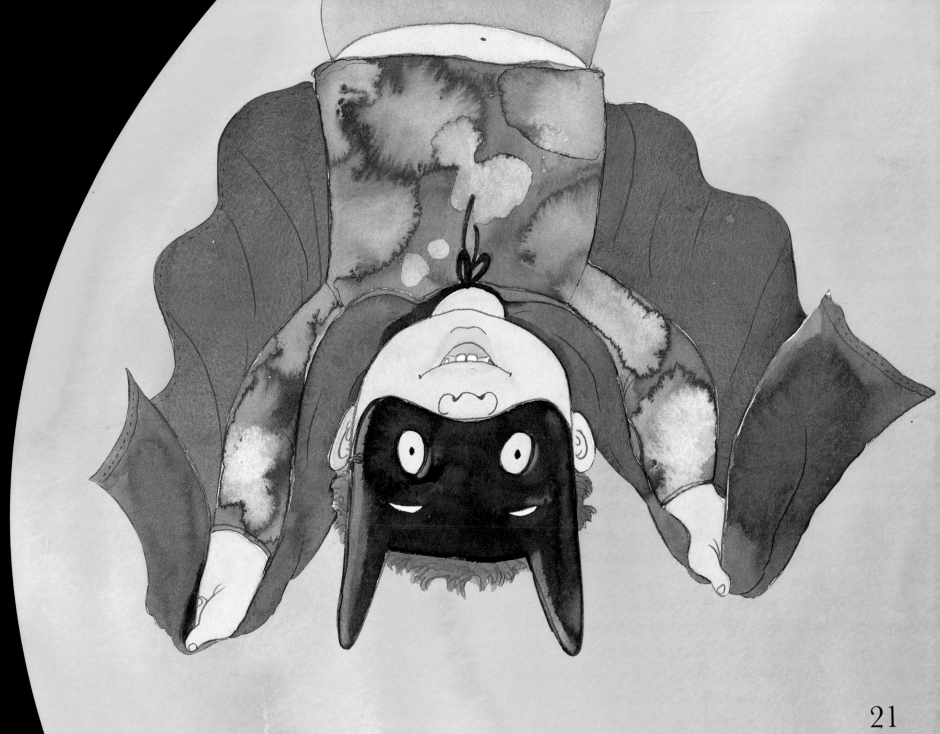

Who could live in a world without wolverines?

Not Anna!
Anna lives in Scandinavia
and she would love to see
a clumsy wolverine
one winter's day –
thumping
through secret,
snowy places.
Wild and free.

Wolverines are the size of dogs! They live in many cold countries. They are hunted for their fur and the large wilderness areas they need to live in are disappearing.

23

我愛熊貓

Who could live in a world without pandas?

Not Chen!
Chen lives in China and he loves pandas. He wishes they could be safe and happy – eating bamboo, sitting in their forests.
Wild and free.

25

Who could live in a world without jaguars?

Not Maria! Maria lives in South America. She hopes the jaguars and the rainforests will soon be protected forever – the jaguar prowling in the rainforest. Wild and free.

26

Protection helps rare animals to survive. Protecting animals means providing quiet places for them to live called nature reserves; passing special laws to stop them being hurt or disturbed by hunters, and making sure they have enough to eat and somewhere safe to raise their babies. To protect an animal population we have also to protect its food and habitat (see pages 2, 9, 13, 24, 26).

Rainforests are huge areas of forest bigger than some European countries. Sometimes they are called 'the earth's lungs' because they give off clouds of the oxygen we all need to breathe (see page 27).

Rare an animal is rare when there there are not many left in a place, or a country or even the whole world (see pages 5, 24).

Species is a word to describe types of animals – like whales or dogs.

Wilderness is large areas of wild country all over the world where people don't live and there are few roads (see page 23).

Wolves are surviving in some parts of the world but in other places they have been wiped out. Farmers shoot them for killing sheep and cattle, but wolves really like to hunt deer and rabbits (see back cover and title page).

31

For Ivor Max Manning

If you would like to know more about animals in danger and how to help visit the website of WWF – the Conservation organisation on www.panda.org. From here you can link to your own country's branch of the WWF.

This edition 2014

First published by Franklin Watts,
338 Euston Road, London NW1 3BH

Franklin Watts Australia,
Level 17 / 207 Kent Street, Sydney NSW 2000

The illustrations in this book were made by Brita and Mick.
Find out more about Mick and Brita at www.mickandbrita.com

Series editor: Paula Borton
Art Director: Robert Walster

A CIP catalogue record is available from the British Library.
Dewey Classification 574.5

Printed in China

ISBN 978 1 4451 2895 5

Franklin Watts is a division of Hachette Children's Books,
an Hachette UK company. www.hachette.co.uk